COVID-19 AND PUBLIC–PRIVATE PARTNERSHIPS IN ASIA AND THE PACIFIC

GUIDANCE NOTE

FEBRUARY 2021

ADB

ASIAN DEVELOPMENT BANK

© 2021 Asian Development Bank
6 ADB Avenue, Mandaluyong City, 1550 Metro Manila, Philippines
Tel +63 2 8632 4444; Fax +63 2 8636 2444
www.adb.org

Some rights reserved. Published in 2021.

ISBN 978-92-9262-585-6 (print); 978-92-9262-586-3 (electronic); 978-92-9262-587-0 (ebook)
Publication Stock No. TIM210040
DOI: http://dx.doi.org/10.22617/TIM210040

The views expressed in this publication are those of the authors and do not necessarily reflect the views and policies of the Asian Development Bank (ADB) or its Board of Governors or the governments they represent.

ADB does not guarantee the accuracy of the data included in this publication and accepts no responsibility for any consequence of their use. The mention of specific companies or products of manufacturers does not imply that they are endorsed or recommended by ADB in preference to others of a similar nature that are not mentioned.

By making any designation of or reference to a particular territory or geographic area, or by using the term "country" in this document, ADB does not intend to make any judgments as to the legal or other status of any territory or area.

Please contact pubsmarketing@adb.org if you have questions or comments with respect to content, or if you wish to obtain copyright permission for your intended use that does not fall within these terms, or for permission to use the ADB logo.

Corrigenda to ADB publications may be found at http://www.adb.org/publications/corrigenda.

Notes:
In this publication, "$" refers to United States dollars.
ADB recognizes "China" as the People's Republic of China.

On the cover: As people adapt to the new normal amidst the pandemic, strict adherence to health and safety protocols in the workplace, in public areas, and even at home is crucial to stem the tide of transmission of the coronavirus disease (COVID-19) (photos by ADB).

Cover design by Anthony C. Villanueva.

Contents

Tables

Abbreviations

ADB	Asian Development Bank
Cth	Commonwealth
CDM	Construction (Design and Management)
COVID-19	coronavirus disease
DMC	developing member country
PPP	public–private partnership
PRC	People's Republic of China
SOP	site operating procedures

Sri Lankan railway workers spray disinfectant inside a train as a preventative measure against coronavirus in Colombo, Sri Lanka. The Sri Lankan government plans to relax island-wide day time curfew imposed for nearly 2 months to restart the country's economic activities (photo by M.A. Pushpa Kumara/Asian Development Bank).

1 Introduction

This guidance note was prepared by a cross-departmental team at the Asian Development Bank (ADB).[1] It is intended to support stakeholders involved in public–private partnership (PPP) projects that have been or will be impacted by the coronavirus disease (COVID-19) pandemic. The ADB team was supported by White & Case LLP, an international law firm, in the preparation of this guidance note.[2]

The COVID-19 pandemic is a major global crisis that requires national, regional, and global intervention. The ADB brief, titled "An Updated Assessment of the Economic Impact of COVID-19", estimated that the potential economic impact on Asia and the Pacific could range from $1.7 trillion to $2.5 trillion (across different containment scenarios).[3] Governments, international finance institutions, and other relevant parties are set to mobilize efforts to mitigate such impact as best as possible. The COVID-19 pandemic has had a wide-ranging impact on the ways in which businesses are able to operate. Social distancing measures have had, and are likely to continue to have, a material impact on productivity and supply chains.

---

[1] The cross-departmental team consists of ADB's Public–Private Partnership Thematic Group (Srinivas Sampath and Sanjay Grover), Governance Thematic Group (Bruno Carrasco and Hanif Rahemtulla), and Office of the General Counsel (Colin Gin, Minh Day, and Zheng Hao Chan).

[2] This guidance note is intended to serve as a guide for ADB's clients or other stakeholders as to what ADB views as relevant considerations for PPP projects amid the effects of COVID-19. It does not constitute advice by ADB or White & Case. The ADB team and its advisors are available to provide project-specific advice and/or any consultation in relation to the points raised in this guidance note.

[3] C. Y. Park et al. 2020. An Updated Assessment of the Economic Impact of COVID-19. *ADB Briefs*. No. 133. Manila: ADB.

The effects of the pandemic are particularly relevant for PPP projects in all stages of the development life cycle. Governments, sponsors, and lenders are making procurement decisions in an environment of some uncertainty and it is important for all stakeholders to understand the key risks. PPP projects in Asia and the Pacific will require careful consideration on this front, particularly with regard to the implementation of quality project preparation practices.[4]

ADB's Strategy 2030 emphasizes the importance of expanding PPPs to help ADB's developing member countries (DMCs) across Asia and the Pacific address the challenges of entrenched poverty and vulnerability, global economic uncertainty, inequality, climate change and environmental degradation, urbanization, and aging.[5] Through assisting with the development, structuring, and preparation of bankable projects, as well as the development of enabling PPP policy and regulations, ADB will work together with its DMCs to create sustainable opportunities for private sector investment and participation, mobilizing a broader range of financial resources. In the context of the COVID-19 pandemic impacts and related considerations discussed in sections 2–5, ADB expects that the importance of such efforts should be reinforced and further tailored to DMCs' evolving requirements.

This paper considers
   (i)   how COVID-19 has impacted PPP projects generally (including projects already under procurement),
   (ii) the contractual implications of COVID-19,
  (iii) how relief can be provided outside of the contractual provisions, and
  (iv) broader government considerations in managing the impact of COVID-19 on PPP projects moving forward.

---

[4] World Bank Group. 2018. *Procuring Infrastructure Public–Private Partnerships Report 2018: Assessing Government Capability to Prepare, Procure, and Manage PPPs*. Washington, DC. Based on an index from 0 to 100 of global best practices for project preparation, East Asia and the Pacific scored 40 compared to an average of 65 for high-income Organisation for Economic Co-operation and Development countries. This demonstrates the need for more work in Asia to bridge the gap between theory and practice when it comes to implementing quality project preparation practices.

[5] ADB. 2018. *Strategy 2030: Achieving a Prosperous, Inclusive, Resilient, and Sustainable Asia and the Pacific*. Manila.

General view of a deserted road in Colombo, Sri Lanka. Sri Lankan government suspended all arriving flights, implemented an island-wide curfew until further notice in the country, and strongly requested people to follow safety measures recommended by health authorities. The election commission announced that the scheduled 2020 general election will be postponed due to the prevailing situation of the coronavirus pandemic (photo by M.A. Pushpa Kumara/Asian Development Bank).

2 Potential Impact of COVID-19 on Public–Private Partnership Projects

COVID-19 has resulted in substantial changes to human interaction across the globe. To curb the spread of the virus, countries continue to restrict entry across their borders and have implemented social distancing measures that inhibit citizens from being in close proximity with each other. Several countries are taking tentative steps to relax these restrictions, but in a conservative fashion out of concern for the risk of subsequent waves of infection.

These measures have had a profound impact on the global economy, with disruptions to supply chains and shrinking demand for products and services. In the context of PPP projects at various stages of progress, each of these elements is considered further in this section.

It is also notable that the impact of COVID-19 may sometimes be occurring against a broader context or market trends of
   (i) decreasing PPP project value and volume,
   (ii) an increasing PPP project risk allocation and assumptions being taken on the private sector side, and
   (iii) a perception on the public sector side that value for money may not currently be realized fully on PPP projects.

Pre-Commercial Operations Stage

Impact on Supply Chains

Notwithstanding the significant increase in automation, the manufacturing and construction sectors still require labor-intensive activities and high levels of workforce interaction. Swathes of factories and work sites deemed nonessential by governments have been ordered to close or curb production activities for significant periods during the COVID-19 pandemic. This poses particular issues for PPP projects yet to reach their commercial operations date.

In contrast to the operations phase of projects, the construction phase is labor-intensive and vulnerable to supply-side impacts such as workplace restrictions for construction workers, the unavailability of materials and equipment, and longer lead times caused by this impact.

In early 2020, when the People's Republic of China (PRC) was among the countries worst affected by the pandemic, suppliers of materials and equipment for PPP projects could not fulfill their orders from factories in the PRC, and looked to Europe and the United States for alternative sources of supply. Shortages included raw materials, key components, and machinery, leading to widespread impacts on all projects and particularly PPPs in the construction phase. For example, bottlenecks in wind power supply chains have created shortages of the key components for wind turbines, which have led to delays. The PRC is estimated to account for 40%–50% of the global wind energy supply chain. Vestas, the world's largest supplier of turbines, and Siemens Gamesa, a Spanish manufacturer, both have assembly facilities in the PRC that were forced to shut down. Both recorded net losses in their midyear results, which was attributed to supply chain disruptions. Since European countries have also ordered mass lockdowns and PRC manufacturing has increased, there has been a pivot back to PRC-sourced materials and equipment, but under a far more constrained supply capacity. While the PRC is particularly referred to in this paragraph on the basis of its occupying a particularly significant space in global supply chains, similar dynamics could also have been observed elsewhere across global supply chain networks because of lockdowns and disruptions across different countries.

Even with the easing of restrictions, many governments are under pressure to revisit the veracity of their supply chains, especially where there may be particular dependence on offshore-sourced goods and materials. While supply chains vary across PPP projects, the impact is more acute for international than domestic supply chains because of drops in international trade volumes, shipping disruptions (e.g., in the PRC, where containers were stranded in ports because of movement restrictions), and delays caused by labor restrictions and inspections.

In PPP projects, governments and proponents alike must be conscious of the need to be agile with respect to the sourcing of materials and equipment.

Impact on the Availability of Expertise

The closure of borders and the general reduction in the availability of international flights during the pandemic mean that it is increasingly difficult to bring from abroad foreign experts to work on-site on complex PPP projects. For example, in some Pacific island nations, it has been virtually impossible to mobilize foreign expertise because of the suspension of flights by commercial airlines.

The extent to which expertise can be made available to PPP projects will dictate the speed and cost at which PPP projects can be completed.

While exceptions to travel bans may be applied for, border and flight restrictions may increase reliance on local workforces and remote working arrangements for those work disciplines that are based upon "desktop" activities. Although some of these effects may be considered a boon for domestic labor forces (e.g., where construction workers are sourced locally), this does not overcome the shortfall in relevant expertise, which is likely to cause material delays to the progress of PPP projects.

Impact on the Manner of Performing Works

The quarantining and social distancing measures being implemented in response to the COVID-19 pandemic necessarily change the way in which works are performed.

For example, in Singapore, a large number of infections have been diagnosed among certain migrant worker dormitories. As a result, affected workers have been housed in quarantine zones. During such quarantine periods, it has not been possible for the quarantined laborers to enter and work on construction sites, and there have been numerous instances where construction sites have been shuttered until the labor force can be remobilized.

Social distancing measures implemented by central governments, and indeed by corporations themselves, have significantly restricted the number of workers that may be colocated on-site at any given time. For example, whereas a site elevator may have previously carried up to 30 people, this number may now be restricted to around 4–6 people in keeping with proximity restrictions. Staggered work hours and workforce rotation have also contributed to a reduction in site productivity.

Infrastructure Demand Profiles

Social distancing and pandemic response measures have changed infrastructure usage and demand patterns worldwide. Many of these changes are likely to persist in coming years.

With greater numbers of people working from home, there has been a substantial reduction in toll road and mass transit patronage. Air and rail travel have materially diminished across national borders and across states and provinces. News reports indicate that leisure travel may not resume until the middle of 2021. This has left airports and travel terminals largely underutilized, which deny those projects their usual source of air-side revenue (such as gate and landing fees) and land-side revenue (such as retail). Social infrastructure, such as sports stadiums, are being used to host sporting events for television broadcast, but without the spectators who would otherwise deliver the operators an important source of revenue: gate fees and food and beverage sales. In the case of existing PPP projects, these changes have significantly affected the underlying economics of these projects. Conversely, there has been increased uptake and traffic for telecommunications infrastructure, as well as personal modes of transport. Health infrastructure is also experiencing increased demand, and higher operational costs are passed through to the government via availability payment adjustments.

The consequences of COVID-19 for the prioritization of future PPP projects are uncertain. Economic experts predict that the resumption of normal economic and social activity, and with it, typical demand for infrastructure, will be dependent on the successful deployment of a vaccine. Regardless of a vaccine, health authorities may look at social distancing measures more broadly, which could change the density of infrastructure usage (e.g., permitted maximum rail carriage densities).

Overall, it has been rare for government-procured projects to be canceled because of COVID-19. There are a number of notable examples of governments directing the slowdown or suspension of government projects: the construction of Terminal 5 of Changi Airport in Singapore being delayed is one such example. However, looking more broadly, governments are generally resisting any delays to PPP projects and are instead looking at ways to expedite them. The reasons for this may include the following:

(i)   PPP projects have long gestation periods. The timeline for procurement of a PPP project can range from 20 to 36 months in experienced markets and many years in less experienced ones; if one were to take into account all of the phases of a PPP project, commencing from policy setting and regulatory due diligence to selection of the winning bidder and implementation, this timeline may stretch even further in some cases. These timelines require governments to take a long-term view (beyond short-term economic cycles), whereas COVID-19, and its financial and contractual implications for these projects, would hopefully be a shorter-term issue in comparison.

(ii) PPP projects (and infrastructure projects, in general) are considered to be a vehicle for effective public investment that can achieve a fiscal multiplier effect, and a key driver of economic stimulus efforts that may catalyze increased fund flows within and across slowing economies and defray poorly performing sectors such as retail, food and beverage, entertainment, and such other sectors that depend upon discretionary spending by customers.[6] Indeed, many governments see the continuation of shovel-ready infrastructure and PPP projects as a feature of their recovery efforts (e.g., PPP program announcements have been made in Australia, the Philippines, the PRC, and Thailand). Noting the need for immediate stimulus, government spending is expected to also focus on smaller-scale projects that might be advanced more quickly.

(iii) Compared to the 2008 global financial crisis, there is anecdotal evidence that the COVID-19 pandemic has not materially affected the availability of credit for PPP projects, with private banks still registering an appetite to lend to quality, creditworthy projects. This observation also applies to lines of credit extended to governments for more bandwidth to support their economies—the level of public sector credit activity has increased overall as a direct response to the effects of the pandemic (though the specific proportion allocated to PPP projects has not yet been confirmed). For example, ADB announced in April 2020 that it is making available more than $18 billion of funding to DMC government borrowers for deployment to support their budgets as a consequence of the economic fallout from COVID-19. These funds can potentially be deployed to defray government costs of supporting PPP projects. To complement these efforts across its sovereign operations, ADB, through its nonsovereign operations, has also committed $1.84 billion to support private sector counterparties.

While government-led projects are often insulated from liquidity shocks, increased government indebtedness is expected to eventually affect the financing of future infrastructure and PPP projects, particularly once the full economic impact of COVID-19 is better understood. This is amplified in cases where the contractual PPP arrangements require governments to make payments under an availability payment structure (particularly for operational facilities), given strains caused by significant pandemic-related drops in governments' tax revenues and user fee collections. Likewise, governments may be forced to deploy available resources to necessary upgrades to existing projects, in priority over new ones, to meet post-COVID-19 requirements for infrastructure usage (e.g., maximum user densities in public transport in accordance with social distancing requirements, and reserved capacity in public hospitals for the isolation of patients with infectious diseases). The uncertain overall environment poses challenges for governments to precisely identify and manage risks, which affects their ability to determine the optimal level of guarantees and other forms of contingent liabilities to be assumed.

---

[6]   Global Infrastructure Hub. 2020 *How Effective Is Public Infrastructure Investment in Supporting COVID-19 Economic Recovery Efforts?* 14 December.

From a broader perspective, economic and financial sustainability, as well as the strengthening of institutions, will be equally important in the context of scarce resources and limited fiscal headroom in the pandemic's immediate aftermath. Emergency financial support should ultimately be integrated into an overall framework that does not jeopardize debt sustainability. In the medium to long term, a sound fiscal framework should be combined with increased investment in high-quality infrastructure that provides direct positive social and economic impact, climate resilience, and more effective delivery of public goods and services. Green investment will also continue to have a positive effect on the speed at which the stimulus delivers economic impact for every dollar invested. Project parties will continue to be challenged as to how they can effectively internalize future returns on an infrastructure project against up-front costs that may be exacerbated by the overall constraints brought about by the COVID-19 pandemic.

Affected Public–Private Partnership Market Participants

Key project proponents, including global construction and design contractors, are affected by the wider economic impact of COVID-19. This is particularly the case given the impact of the user-based demand outlined in the preceding section (Infrastructure Demand Profiles).

There is potential for some consolidation of market participants in response to COVID-19, particularly since smaller market participants may find it harder to compete in a rapidly changing and uncertain environment. Similarly, it may be expected that there is less flexibility regarding achievable risk allocations.

In addition to principals, sponsors, and lenders, the pandemic is likely to affect additional stakeholders such as insurers. Governments should be mindful of the likely impacts on traditional construction, property, and professional liability insurance policies, and whether future policies will need to be adapted.

Similarly, governments are likely to face different and increased fiscal risks as a result of the pandemic. As is noted throughout this guidance note, uncertainty with respect to government receipts creates the need for governments to identify and assess fiscal risks appropriately in order to manage them effectively. A sound legal and administrative framework is crucial for this exercise. While regional administrative frameworks differ, a fiscal risk matrix could be developed by governments to coordinate risk management between finance ministries, the executive branch of central governments, and each relevant government department.

Procurement processes should be mindful of these additional pressures on participants to ensure that bidding for new PPP projects remains competitive and achieves efficient outcomes.

Table 1 presents this section's summary of key findings and recommendations.

Table 1: Section 2 Summary—Potential Impact of COVID-19 on Public–Private Partnership Projects

Key Findings	Recommendations
• PPP projects and project participants may be affected by changes in supply chain, human resources, and work arrangements. • Projects in the construction phase have been more vulnerable to and more affected by supply-side impact and have experienced longer lead times. • Infrastructure demand profiles have changed significantly but have affected assets differently and are likely to persist. Mass transit, air, and rail patronage has decreased significantly because of COVID-19 restrictions and measures, while there has been an increase in demand for telecom and healthcare infrastructure. • Despite challenges and consequences of COVID-19, governments generally continue looking to infrastructure projects, including PPPs, as a key driver of economic stimulus and recovery. • Unlike the 2008 global financial crisis, the COVID-19 crisis has not had the same impact on availability of credit thus far. For example, ADB has increased lending in response to COVID-19.	• Governments and other PPP project participants should remain mindful of their respective short-, medium-, and long-term outlook toward PPP projects and programs. • In the short to medium term, responsiveness and agility will be key to adapting existing projects to ongoing changes. In the medium to long term, enhanced and broader policy and administrative frameworks should sustainably support coordination and risk allocation across governments and PPP project participants. • Governments may want to consider smaller-scale projects that might be advanced more quickly if the goal is to accelerate economic recovery. • Governments must identify and assess fiscal risks to manage consequences of COVID-19, such as uncertainty with respect to government receipts. Governments should consider developing a fiscal risk matrix to coordinate risk management between finance ministries, the executive branch of central governments, and each relevant government department.

ADB = Asian Development Bank, COVID-19 = coronavirus disease, PPP = public–private partnership.
Source: ADB.

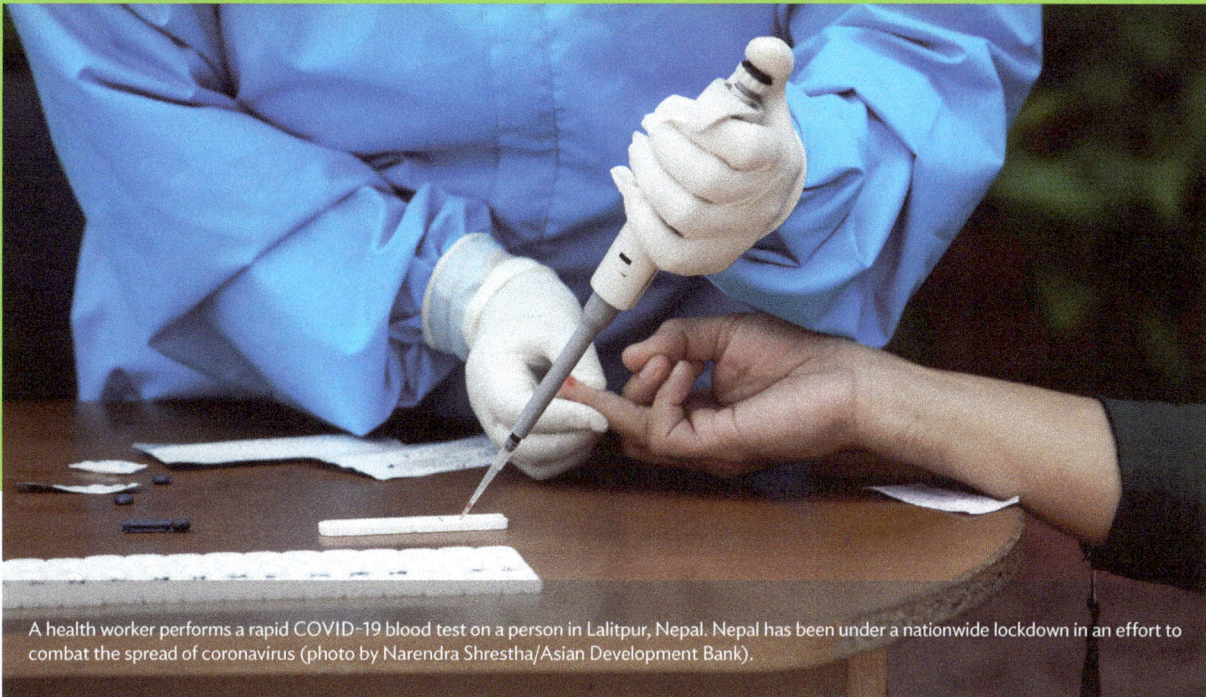

A health worker performs a rapid COVID-19 blood test on a person in Lalitpur, Nepal. Nepal has been under a nationwide lockdown in an effort to combat the spread of coronavirus (photo by Narendra Shrestha/Asian Development Bank).

3 Impact of COVID-19 on Existing Contractual Risk Allocations

The examples set out in section 2 of the various ways in which COVID-19 has affected the PPP projects are not exhaustive. PPP market participants are likely affected based on their individual circumstances. However, there appear to be three broad categories of COVID-19 impact:

(i) circumstances arising directly from COVID-19, e.g., incapacity of workforce because of infection;

(ii) additional expenses incurred to keep the facility running and available, while ensuring the facility meets new health and safety requirements and social distancing norms; and

(iii) changes in circumstances in reaction to COVID-19, e.g., legally imposed isolation to minimize the risk of the spread of COVID-19.

Drawing upon examples from a range of PPP contracts in multiple sectors across different jurisdictions, it may be possible to present a generalized explanation of the types of contractual relief that affected parties to a PPP contract may seek as a consequence of COVID-19.

There are four avenues of relief that may be relevant for COVID-19 impact and the types of relief that an affected party may seek. These are shown in Table 2 and are discussed in turn in this section.

Table 2: Avenues of Contractual Relief

Avenue of Relief	Type of Relief		
	Extension of Time	Compensation	Termination Rights
Natural force majeure events	Yes	Depends on specific provisions in the relevant public–private partnership (PPP) contract, and applicable limited categories (e.g., debt service costs not met by insurances)	Yes, by either party (after a prolonged period)
General changes in law	Yes	No compensation	No
Discriminatory changes in law (targeting industry or PPP project)	Yes	Increased costs and delay costs	Yes, by PPP contractor (and sometimes the procuring agency) (after a prolonged period)
Scope changes	Yes	Increased costs and delay costs	No

Source: Asian Development Bank.

Natural Force Majeure Events

Legal Concept of Force Majeure

Force majeure differs from the doctrine of frustration, which is an English common law concept. Frustration occurs when an event happens that so radically and fundamentally changes the nature of the parties' contractual arrangements that it would be unjust to hold them to their obligations. The contract is deemed void and the parties are discharged from their obligations. In practice, frustration is rare and very difficult to prove.

In contrast to frustration, force majeure is not defined in the common law or under English statutes, and is entirely a creature of contract. However, many jurisdictions contain statutory definitions of force majeure (e.g., in civil law systems), and it is important to check whether this applies to individual projects (notwithstanding the contractual regime). It follows that a close examination of the specific contractual provisions is required to ascertain the likely impact of COVID-19 in a force majeure context.

Contractual regimes regarding "natural" force majeure are typically intended to supplant the common law of frustration and, in that respect, are considered to be "no-fault" events. Consequently, PPP contracts will usually give an affected party relief from their obligations to the extent impacted by an event recognized as a force majeure event under the PPP contract.

Typically, a claim of force majeure requires the occurrence of an event beyond the contracting parties' control and that causes either party to be unable to perform its obligations. In some cases, the relevant event must be unforeseeable, though this would be unusual given most force majeure events are technically "foreseeable" even if unlikely. In most cases, a robust contractual regime requires the relevant event to meet certain criteria.

Where a force majeure event is established, the affected party is usually excused from its obligations to the extent they are affected by the event.

Scope of Force Majeure Events

In many PPP contracts across multiple industry sectors (including airport and rail concessions, water treatment build-operate-transfer projects, and power purchase agreements), epidemics and pandemics are expressly listed as force majeure events and entitle the affected party relief from its performance obligations to the extent actually impacted by the epidemic or pandemic. In some instances where epidemic or pandemic is not listed, there have nevertheless been "catch-all" provisions that classify as a force majeure event any event affecting the PPP project that was not foreseen at the time of contracting and that is beyond the reasonable control of the affected party.

Interestingly, in a rail concession in Australia, the classification of force majeure events was limited to an exhaustive list, which excluded any reference to epidemic or pandemic. However, the list did include "biological contamination," which might arguably apply in the context of COVID-19 infections.

Force Majeure Relief

The most common forms of relief for force majeure events are nonmonetary ones, such as
  (i) extensions of time commensurate with the delay for the PPP contractor to bring the works to commercial operation;
  (ii) relaxation from compliance with key performance indicators and performance standards for affected operations; and
  (iii) an extension of the overall PPP contract term in lieu of monetary compensation (the logic being that the PPP contractor may have more time to recover from any shortfall in revenue via the extended period); this entitlement is usually curbed to the extent that the PPP contractor has been able to offset its lost revenues from other mitigation strategies, such as business interruption insurance.

Procurement agencies (e.g., in Australia, Central Asia, and the Philippines) are readily willing to accept these forms of nonmonetary relief, but can be assertive in negotiations over payment of compensation. This is where the contrast between various PPP contracts becomes most apparent. For example, some power purchase agreements that are dependent on variable energy payments do not allow the electricity suppliers to receive compensation for any shortfall in revenue because of events such as COVID-19 affecting the operations of their plant. On the other hand, PPP contracts that have multiple categories of payments in their tariff structure and, importantly, that emphasize availability or capacity of the PPP project (such as transport and social infrastructure concessions) more often contain special provisions enabling PPP contractors limited payment so as to preserve the PPP contractor's solvency.

In the worst-case scenario, the affected parties are commonly permitted to terminate the PPP contract in the event that the impact of the force majeure event endures beyond a specific period (which can range from 6 to 18 months depending on the size, complexity, and duration of the PPP project). However, as noted in section 5, termination is often undesirable and expensive and should form a last resort after other strategies have been undertaken.

Practical Considerations of Force Majeure

As illustrated earlier in this section, force majeure may be given differing treatment across jurisdictions and is often specific to the provisions of individual contracts. This poses a particular issue in PPP projects, given the multiple contracting arrangements required. Using a hypothetical example, restrictions on the movement of goods in one country may constitute a force majeure event in a supply contract between a subcontractor and its local supplier. However, this event may not constitute a force majeure event in the contract between the subcontractor and the main contractor, leaving the subcontractor disadvantaged and contractually exposed, and putting the PPP project at risk. Importantly, this negatively affects all parties to the PPP projects.

Such a "mismatch" scenario is particularly relevant in the context of COVID-19 disruptions, notwithstanding such a chain of events would likely be borne out over a significant period of time. Certainly, the full impact of the pandemic, in this respect, are yet to be fully observed. To avoid potential supply chain disruptions along the chain, it is important to effectively arrange and appropriately draft "back-to-back" contracts in the PPP contract suite to the maximum extent possible.[7] While jurisdictional issues may be an unavoidable risk given some statutory regimes, creating a robust framework will provide parties with maximum certainty in the contractual context.

In addition, it is crucial that contracting parties are aware of, and comply with, the relevant notice and mitigation provisions under the PPP contract in order to avoid further contractual issues.

Changes in Law

What Qualifies as a Change in Law?

In response to the COVID-19 pandemic, governments around the world have been enacting social distancing and other pandemic response measures. To the extent that it has been necessary to implement new laws to give effect to such measures, and where these laws were enacted after a PPP contract took effect, PPP contracts generally tend to be quite clear about the PPP contractor being entitled to claim relief and, subject to the terms of the PPP contract, compensation.

However, in many locations, existing legislation provides for the declaration of a "pandemic" or similar event, which gives rise to broad emergency powers—all within the existing laws. Furthermore, wide-reaching impact of COVID-19 across economies have compelled government health and labor agencies to implement specific guidelines for particular industries and sectors (e.g., the regimented restart of the Singaporean construction sector regulated by the Building and Construction Authority). While such guidelines may not have the force of law, it is common that a PPP contractor will be contractually required to comply with them, unless directed otherwise.

In such cases where no new law has actually been enacted, the right of an affected party to claim relief or compensation because of the declaration is less clear and may depend on whether the relevant PPP contract has incorporated regulations or rulings of this nature in the change of law regime. It is important for contracting parties to consider these additional measures given the potential cost implications that may follow.

Actions to mitigate COVID-19 risks on a PPP project may be viewed as a necessary part of the PPP contractor's existing contractual obligations. PPP contracts typically provide for a near-complete transfer of occupational health and safety risk to the PPP contractor, and for PPP contractors to perform their obligations in accordance with best practices. Actions taken by PPP contractors in accordance with their health and safety obligations, or otherwise as required for best practice, may have changed because of COVID-19 risks, but not the underlying law.

Distinction between General and Discriminatory Changes in Law

There are numerous examples where PPP contracts seek to draw a distinction between general changes in law (i.e., laws that apply equally across industries) and discriminatory changes in law that target either the PPP project or one of its contract parties and have an adverse effect on the PPP project and its economics. In the strictest of cases (such as some Philippine transport concessions and South Asian liquefied natural gas terminal use

---

[7] Back-to-back contracts are contractual arrangements, whereby a primary contracting party seeks to pass on obligations and liabilities pursuant to the main contract to the subcontracting parties under the relevant subcontract.

agreements), only discriminatory changes in law qualify for performance relief and compensation to be paid to PPP contractors. In other instances (such as rail concessions in Melbourne), the PPP contractor is entitled to such relief and compensation for discriminatory changes in law during both the construction and operations phases of the PPP contract, but only for general changes in law occurring during the operations phase. However, in frontier and emerging markets (such as in Central Asia), governments tend to be more lenient with their relief provisions and allow a contractor to claim compensation if there is a general change in law after the PPP contract is signed.

PPP contractors are required to mitigate their losses, and failure to do so will disentitle the PPP contractor to such relief. In that context, it is important that the procuring agency remains informed regarding the COVID-19 actions actually being taken by the PPP contractor, so that the reasonableness of those measures can be considered and, if necessary, challenged. This is particularly important with respect to a government's exercise of its general emergency powers compared to substantive changes in legislation, and the associated costs from compliance.

The PPP contractor's compliance with the contractual claim procedures should also be monitored by the procuring agency or, if provided for in the relevant PPP contract, by independent auditors and/or engineers.

Scope Changes

From a legal perspective, changes to the PPP scope are typically thought of as being a change to the physical properties of the PPP project, i.e., the permanent works constructed for the PPP project. For example, in many Asian jurisdictions, governments have directed PPP contractors to repurpose medical and other public facilities for use as triage and isolation wards for COVID-19 patients. This situation will typically result in the PPP contractor having some form of performance relief or payment adjustment that takes into account the substitution of works and services arising from the procuring agency's direction.

However, the discussion becomes more complicated when analyzing the parties' rights in respect of any changes to the way in which the works or services are to be performed (e.g., the introduction of new, restrictive working methods or procedures that were not contemplated previously). Legal commentators generally note that PPP contractor relief is not assured and that the prevailing laws and the express wording of the PPP contract must be carefully examined. Nonetheless, it is premature to comment on the tangible effects of these specific scope changes, which are still being borne out.

Delay Events

Non-compensable and compensable delay events refer to events that do not typically change the works to be performed, but rather cause delay or disruption to them. While non-compensable delay events will entitle a PPP contractor to an extension of time, compensable delay events entitle the PPP contractor to an extension of time as well as a claim to its increased site preliminaries and financing costs associated with the delay.

During the operating phase, compensable delay events will commonly entitle the PPP contractor to suspend the performance of their obligations to the extent they are impacted, and to have their additional costs paid.

In the context of COVID-19, the most probable compensable delay events that may occur are
- (i) acts of omissions of the principal or procuring authority (or its associates) in connection with the PPP project, and
- (ii) delays to interfacing parties (e.g., delays to other contractors).

Particularly, where the state (or other government entity) is the procuring agency, it is probable that the state will be taking a range of actions in respect of COVID-19. In that case, the procuring agency's defense to a claim will be that such actions are not taken in respect of the PPP project, but rather are implemented more broadly across the economy.

Where interfacing parties are also delayed by COVID-19, and that causes delay to the PPP contractor, then that delay may also be claimable by the PPP contractor. That being said, whether such relief is available is entirely dependent on the contractual terms. In some cases, the PPP contractor will have assumed the risk of delays caused by interfacing parties; and, in those circumstances, the PPP contractor will not be entitled to make a claim against the procuring agency (although it may have recourse to the interfacing party).

Table 3 presents this section's summary of key findings and recommendations.

Table 3: Section 3 Summary—Impact of COVID-19 on Existing Contractual Risk Allocations

Key Findings	Recommendations
• COVID-19 generally has impacted projects in three broad categories: (i) circumstances arising directly from COVID-19, such as incapacity of workforce because of infection; (ii) additional expenses incurred to keep the facility running and available; and (iii) changes in circumstances in reaction to COVID-19, such as legally imposed isolation to minimize the risk of the spread of COVID-19. • Generally, there are four avenues of relief in PPP contracts that are most relevant to an affected PPP contract party: contractual relief arrangements for (i) natural force majeure events, (ii) general changes in law, (iii) discriminatory changes in law, and (iv) scope changes, each of which may grant or trigger time relief, compensation, or termination rights. Each must be assessed separately against the impact of COVID-19 on the affected party. • Applicable relief for delay events may also be taken into consideration.	• PPP contract termination is often undesirable and expensive, and should form a last resort after other strategies have been undertaken. • Parties must identify mismatch scenarios, such as supply chain disruptions along the chain and across jurisdictions, and try to effectively arrange "back-to-back" contracts in the PPP contract suite to manage those risks. • It is crucial that PPP contract parties are aware of, and comply with, the relief provisions in PPP contracts, particularly the relevant notice and mitigation provisions. • Compliance with contractual claim procedures should be monitored by the procuring agency or, if provided for in the PPP contract, by independent auditors or engineers. • Governments must be aware of actions taken by contractors in response to the claimed effects of COVID-19, evaluate the reasonableness of such response or consider grounds for challenging such response, and ensure that the contractor has complied with obligations to mitigate losses. • Governments must evaluate the appropriate relief provisions for COVID-19 impact, based on jurisdiction and local practices, as there will not be a uniform approach applicable across all DMCs and assets. As part of their evaluation process, governments must be aware of the various approaches to address COVID-19 impact and relevant relief provisions, from providing relief and compensation for discriminatory changes in law during the construction and operations phases of the PPP contract to granting more lenient relief provisions and compensation for general changes in law.

COVID-19 = coronavirus disease, DMC = developing member country, PPP = public–private partnership.
Source: Asian Development Bank.

Passengers walk wearing protective mask as they travel via train at the platform of the national railway station at Kamlapur in Dhaka, Bangladesh (photo by Asian Development Bank).

4 Government Contracting Responses to COVID-19

Each of the risk regimes outlined in section 3 is intended to apply in the case of unknown risks. Clearly, the COVID-19 pandemic is a known risk for parties currently negotiating contracts, although the nature and duration of its impact are uncertain. In this section, practical steps for contractual risk management are set out, alongside the key considerations for the risk allocation under PPP contracts currently being negotiated.

Managing the Risk of an Increase in COVID-19 Impacts

The Contractual Approach

If a new PPP project is procured today, it may be expected, and indeed unavoidable, that prospective PPP contractors would bid a risk allocation, program, and price that assume a level of disruption because of COVID-19.

In contrast, procuring agencies might be inclined to insist that bidders fully price COVID-19 risks on the basis of a pre-COVID-19 PPP contract template that seeks to transfer as much of that risk as possible onto the prospective PPP contractors. However, it may be doubtful that this will be achievable. Going forward, it is likely that parties to PPPs will need to ensure their base case financial models to take into effect the impact of COVID-19 as well as similar events.

For instance, procuring agencies make assumptions regarding forecast demand, and demand for certain commodities may remain depressed, or further deteriorate, depending on how economies recover post-COVID-19. As noted in section 2 (under Public–Private Partnership Projects in their Pre-Commercial Operations Stage: Impact on Supply Chains), the impact is likely widespread and varied across PPP projects. The supply of materials and equipment will affect all construction projects, but there may be sector-specific impact, such as thermal power generation facilities dependent on feedstock commodities. The same principles apply to revenues linked to user-fee concessions, such as toll roads and other transport PPP projects.

While the availability-based payment structures commonly found in operational social PPP projects are likely to be more immune to COVID-19-related impact (notwithstanding the increased pressure on health PPPs, and the possible non-use of some education PPPs because of school closures), uncertainty surrounding future changes to social dynamics may create a new category of risk for future PPP projects, such as those involving schools and hospitals. These risks will need to be taken into account when these projects are priced. Physical distancing measures may continue to be in place (in some form) , and designs for PPP projects (including retrofitting existing infrastructure) may need to be revisited to cater for the physical requirements of these rules, which will necessarily require a reexamination of PPP payment structures and pricing.

Such risks are more difficult to allocate. A mechanism that reduces the committed offtake (including with respect to availability payments) will significantly affect a PPP project's financial model.

If procuring agencies are able to assume a level of offtaker risk, then that may be an efficient solution to ensuring the PPP project can proceed with the support of its other proponents.

Practical Steps for Contract Management

It is possible (and indeed likely) that contracting parties are unable to fully contract out of the varied implications of the COVID-19 pandemic, the extent of which is still unknown. In these circumstances, it is crucial that contracting parties adhere strictly to the core contractual provisions likely to be affected (as identified in section 3). This includes complying with notice requirements and other administrative matters as they relate to scope changes, changes in law, delay events, and force majeure events. Ensuring there is a robust paper trail of documentation is of critical importance should parties seek to rely on these rights, and in the event of a future dispute.

Best practice for contract management should entail future-proofing PPP contracts to enable projects to meet the known and unknown challenges the pandemic's uncertainty presents. For new PPP projects or the amendment of existing contracts, there is merit in revisiting some contractual mechanics that may previously have been glossed over in negotiations, particularly boilerplate clauses. For example, in order to "COVID-19-proof" a contract's notice provisions, it will be important to ensure the electronic service of notices is accommodated. Similarly, parties may wish to reconsider jurisdiction provisions setting a preferred disputes forum, and whether the drafting caters for virtual dispute resolution in the event courts in a particular jurisdiction are closed.

Managing the Risk of a Reduction in COVID-19 Impacts

As mentioned in the preceding section (Managing the Risk of an Increase in COVID-19 Impacts), it is expected that prospective PPP contractors would bid a risk allocation, program, and price that assume a level of disruption because of COVID-19. A procuring agency may accept this outcome, and be comfortable that they may later issue a change order or an acceleration direction in the event the impact of COVID-19 subsides (e.g., when broad community immunization has been effected). The suitability of this approach will depend on the nature of the PPP and the specific project circumstances; it is likely to be more feasible for smaller projects with inherently higher levels of flexibility.

As an alternative, procuring agencies may seek to pre-agree to the manner in which the program and pricing might be adjusted once the COVID-19 impact subsides.

A procuring agency could request that prospective PPP contractors provide an undisrupted program or price (or both) alongside their COVID-19-disrupted program or price, with a mechanism for the undisrupted program or price to come into effect when the impact of COVID-19 have subsided. This approach may be too rigid to respond to an incremental reduction in COVID-19 restrictions. Such an approach may also increase bid costs, and it is doubtful that the undisrupted program or price (or both) would fully exclude the impact of COVID-19. PPP contractors may be inclined to include additional contingency in the undisrupted program or price (or both) on the basis that it may be more difficult to evaluate, or otherwise that it might be given less weighting during tender evaluation.

Instead, a specific scope changes regime might be considered, which may include the following features:
- (i) the preparation of a revised program at the time the impact of COVID-19 subsides;
- (ii) an independent evaluation of that revised program; and
- (iii) a fixed pricing regime to be applied to the revised program; particularly, since reduction in the COVID-19 impact could be considered a "known" change in scope, lower site preliminaries and margins might be negotiated compared to a typical change in scope.

Table 4 presents this section's summary of key findings and recommendations.

Table 4: Section 4 Summary—Government Contracting Responses to COVID-19

Key Findings	Recommendations
For new PPP projects, prospective PPP project participants will take into account current and forecast factors affected by the COVID-19 pandemic (e.g., demand forecasts, implementation costs, macroeconomic environment) and price bids accordingly. These may lead to increased costs, or changes to project design or implementation, that could require risk allocation considerations.	PPP project parties should work together to agree on how best to incorporate the impact of COVID-19 and similar events on forecasts and financial models. PPP contract parties may look to future-proof PPP contracts (and broader PPP programming) with enhanced mechanisms that will facilitate flexibility and responsiveness to changes over the life of the PPP project. PPP contract parties may also mutually consider and evaluate specific scope changes regimes incorporating program or pricing revisions.

COVID-19 = coronavirus disease, PPP = public–private partnership.
Source: Asian Development Bank.

Workers constructing a hospital for infected COVID-19 patients in Nur-Sultan, Kazakhstan (photo by Turar Kazangapov/ Asian Development Bank).

5 Noncontractual Relief and Other Considerations

Notwithstanding the contractual outcomes, all PPP project participants are expected to be under increased pressure to deliver on their contractual obligations. It is important that procuring agencies recognize those pressures when deciding what actions to take in respect to claims or other PPP project issues. Significant actions (such as declarations of breach and/or events of default) are generally yet to be taken by procuring authorities. This may reflect a desire for project counterparties to seek the resolution of matters without recourse to a dispute, and also the long lead times associated with these processes. Accordingly, the guidance in this section sets out certain best practices (noncontractual) for ensuring PPP projects are protected from the effects of COVID-19. From a broader perspective, it is also important to highlight the importance of

   (i)   quality PPP contract design and risk allocation that will facilitate effective and flexible implementation of the PPP project across the relevant contract parties; and

   (ii) strong legal, regulatory, and institutional frameworks that facilitate fiscal soundness and enable the efficient implementation and management of PPP projects in accordance with best practices.

Maintaining a Strong Relationship with Counterparties

If a PPP contractor is unable to finish the construction of a PPP project on time because of COVID-19, it may be in the procuring agency's interest to help facilitate the completion of the PPP contractor's works, rather than take enforcement action. The Cabinet Office of the Government of the United Kingdom has recognized the importance of this cooperation, issuing an action note in March 2020 urging procurement authorities to maintain supplier payments in the interest of the working relationship and the project. This is to be read in conjunction with the Infrastructure and Projects Authority, which has incorporated the note in its guidance.

A procuring agency should be conscious of a PPP contractor's solvency in the context of COVID-19. If the procuring agency issues breach notices, such notices may have implications for the PPP's financing in circumstances where the financiers may be unable or unwilling to take a lenient approach.

An insolvent PPP contractor is typically of little assistance to a procuring agency and a level of moderation may be necessary in exercising contractual rights. It is prudent, in this case, to map out the legal and commercial implications of alternative approaches to provide a proper risk assessment. While government parties may be tempted take protective action, such as calling on performance security, it is often not in the best interest of the project to resort to such measures.

Given the uncertainty surrounding the full impact of the pandemic, government parties should be proactive in reaching out to existing PPP partners to maintain an open dialogue and working relationship. Maintaining ongoing discussions and dialogue across governments, PPP advisors, and participants can help governments in reviewing PPPs in the worst-affected sectors (primarily transport) to understand the likely demand- and supply-side impact on each PPP project, and to develop a pragmatic solution that ensures continued service delivery to its citizens.

Creating an action plan or agreed set of principles to guide the PPP parties' approach to the pandemic may be an effective starting point for this type of engagement. Such plans can and should be aligned with strategic governmental priorities. Risk mitigation must be a priority in these circumstances, given the significant impact PPP failure would bring for many PPP projects, particularly in emerging market economies.

Extending Additional Support

In times of uncertainty, PPP participants and PPP contractors are often advised to seek renegotiation and amendments to project documents. While governments should maintain an open approach and collaborate with their PPP partners to the maximum extent possible, it is also important, when taking a moderated approach, that procuring agencies take care to reserve their rights and do not let performance security expire without replacement.

It may be possible for governments to extend support to PPP contractors while maintaining a prudent approach. For example, some of these support measures may potentially involve the issuance of financial guarantees to lenders under critical PPP projects, or the redirection of certain payments to PPP special purpose vehicles in order to maintain liquidity. Financial support (with strict conditions and clear time limits) is an important means of ensuring that construction and operating programs remain on track.

While governments may choose to explore all options at this time, it is important to adopt a prudent approach that takes into account demand- and supply-side considerations to the maximum extent possible.

There may also be legislation in place that provides PPP contractors with temporary relief from enforcement actions by procuring agencies in cases where a PPP contractor is impacted by COVID-19. For example, Singapore enacted the COVID-19 (Temporary Measures) Act 2020 in April 2020, under which temporary relief from enforcement actions may be provided to businesses that are unable to fulfill their contractual obligations because of COVID-19. Construction and supply contracts (and bonds or bond equivalents granted under such contracts) fall within the ambit of the act. While enforcement action in active projects is unlikely to have taken place so soon after the onset of COVID-19, this regime has meant that some Singapore law-governed projects have been granted additional protection.

Streamlining Regulatory Processes

Governments may also offer to procuring agencies and PPP contractors further PPP project implementation assistance by legislating and effecting fast-tracked approvals and streamlined conditions for PPP projects. This can serve two key purposes:
  (i) to mobilize shovel-ready PPP projects as quickly as possible to boost employment in the construction sector, and
  (ii) to reduce the time and resources required by PPP participants for the often laborious and lengthy approvals processes imposed on PPP projects.

Such an initiative was introduced in Western Australia in August 2020, where the state government is seeking bilateral action with the Government of Australia on measures to eradicate duplicate environmental approvals and to create a single step approval process (meaning state and federal environmental approvals can be achieved in a unitary manner).

Table 5 presents this section's summary of key findings and recommendations.

Table 5: Section 5 Summary—Noncontractual Relief and Other Considerations

Key Findings	Recommendations
◎ Close coordination across PPP project parties will support effective management of ongoing changes in PPP projects. ◎ Governments have taken varied and broad approaches outside of the relevant PPP contracts to support PPP projects and participants, including enacting legislation granting temporary relief from enforcement action to PPP contractors impacted by COVID-19 and streamlining applicable regulatory and administrative processes.	◎ Creating an action plan or agreed set of principles can help guide the PPP parties' approach and coordination. ◎ Any additional support or streamlined process should ideally be integrated into the broader and longer-term development of sustainable (i) legal, regulatory, and institutional frameworks that facilitate fiscal soundness and enable the efficient implementation and management of PPP projects, in accordance with best practices; and (ii) quality PPP contract design risk allocation that will facilitate effective and flexible implementation of the PPP project across parties. ◎ Governments must be proactive in managing, reaching out to, and supporting their PPP counterparties, since (i) an insolvent concessionaire will not benefit the government, (ii) assistance to a delayed contractor may be more fruitful to the government than an enforcement action for the delay, and (iii) maintenance of ongoing and open discussions with all PPP participants to understand the likely impact of COVID-19 on supply and demand is important in developing a pragmatic solution.

COVID-19 = coronavirus disease, PPP = public–private partnership.
Source: Asian Development Bank.

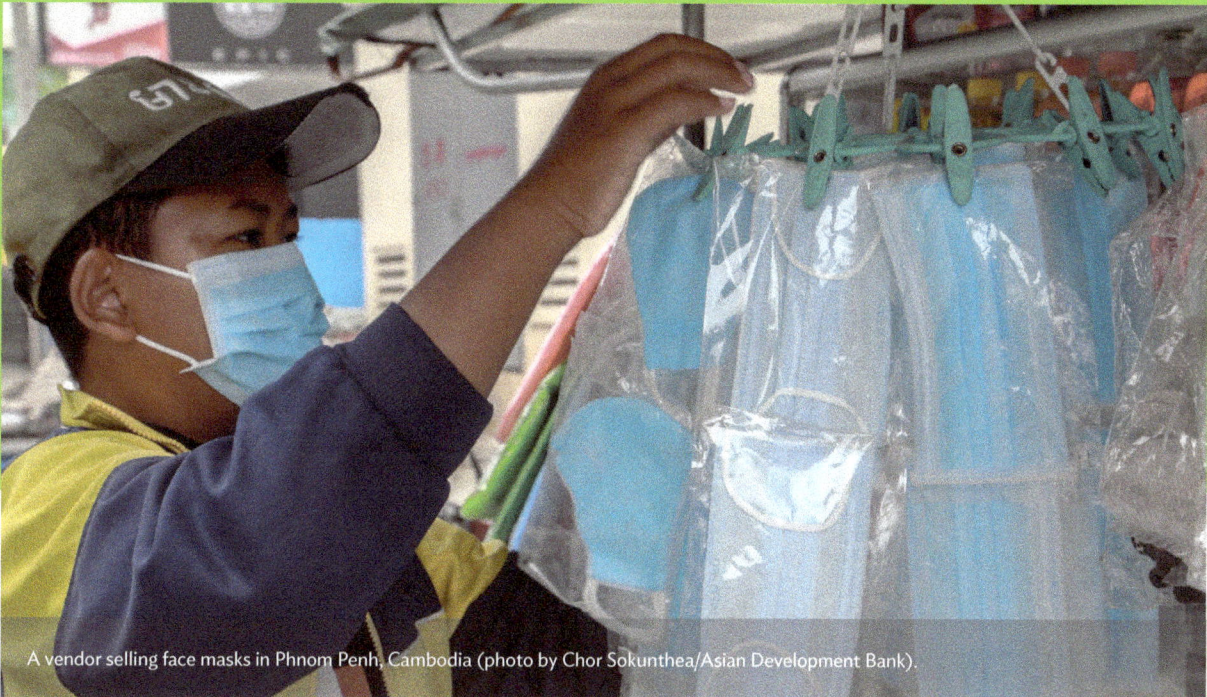
A vendor selling face masks in Phnom Penh, Cambodia (photo by Chor Sokunthea/Asian Development Bank).

6 Conclusion

As the circumstances and impact of COVID-19 continue to evolve in different ways across DMCs, each government and other PPP project parties should continue to closely monitor and assess the short-, medium-, and long-term impacts to PPP projects and programming, and the contractual and noncontractual considerations for each relevant PPP project and contract.

Throughout this process, close coordination and communication across PPP project parties should ultimately support the effective management by the government of PPP projects and programs across ongoing changes in the project or program lifetime. Ultimately, this may lead to the development of sustainable, long-term approaches and frameworks for PPP project and program management.

Appendix
Case Studies

1   Case Studies Regarding Modification Clauses

Australia

On 18 March 2020, COVID-19 was declared to be a human biosecurity emergency under the *Biosecurity Act 2015* (Cth).[1] That declaration entitles the health minister to determine any requirement that he or she deems as necessary to prevent or control the spread of COVID-19.

Noting that such actions are taken under existing law, a public–private partnership (PPP) contractor would be challenged to argue a declaration to be a change in law and to claim relief as a consequence. Particularly, based on the Partnerships Victoria standard Project Deed, there are two kinds of "changes in law" that may entitle the PPP contractor to relief: "general changes in law" and "project-specific changes in law." The actions taken under the *Biosecurity Act 2015* (Cth) are not considered to be changes in law. In any case, even if new laws are enacted, such laws may be expected to be in the nature of a general change in law, rather than one that applies specifically to the project or industry. In that case, the typical risk allocation for general changes in law will only entitle a PPP contractor to relief where the change occurs after practical completion (i.e., during the operating phase of the project).

However, on 28 March 2020, the Department of Health and Human Services of the Victorian State Government in Australia issued a guideline entitled "Best practice for managing construction sites in the COVID-19 environment." Although not a binding guideline, it has been observed that procuring agencies have directed their contractors to comply with such government guidelines within the powers given to the procuring agencies under their PPP contracts to require such adoption. In such circumstances, claims for a change in law, or otherwise, as a change order, are the most probable avenue of claim for PPP contracts in Australia. While the COVID-19 pandemic continues, it is not yet certain which claims PPP contractors will seek to establish, or how successful those claims may be.

Pacific Island Nations

In an ongoing PPP project involving a Pacific island nation, the issue of the impact of a change in law arising from COVID-19 on the PPP contractor was considered at length by the procuring agency. While the granting of relief to the PPP contractor for a failure to achieve the necessary deadlines as a result of COVID-19 was acceptable to the procuring authority, the procuring authority did not consider it reasonable to grant cost relief to the PPP contractor, including if there has been a change in law affecting the PPP contractor as a result of COVID-19. The right for the PPP contractor to seek any form of compensation as a result of COVID-19 was expressly excluded.

---

[1]   References to "Cth" denote the federal (Commonwealth) level of legislation in Australia.

Singapore

The concept of change in law in Singapore PPP contracts is defined very narrowly. Under these PPP contracts, change in law must be a new law representing an addition to, or amendment of, existing laws, or a change in the manner in which a law is applied or interpreted, and which applies expressly to the relevant industry, the project, or the PPP contractor. It may therefore be arguable as to whether any general legislation enacted as a result of COVID-19 would constitute a change in law, entitling the PPP contractor to compensation under the relevant PPP contract.

Before the affected party is entitled to change in law relief, the impact of the change in law would typically have to meet a certain threshold (e.g., net costs or savings of a certain amount per contract year). The parties will agree upon any changes to the PPP contract or to the tariff payment to ensure that the PPP contractor receives the same project return as if the costs arising out of the change in law had not been incurred.

United Kingdom

The Government of the United Kingdom has imposed some changes as part of new legislation (e.g., Coronavirus Act 2020). However, most changes to site working practices arise from the guidance issued by government bodies, such as the Department for Business, Energy & Industrial Strategy's document titled "Working safely during coronavirus (COVID-19)," published on 11 May 2020 and updated on 19 May 2020. It states that firms should follow sector advice, which for the construction industry means the Construction Leadership Council's Site Operating Procedures (SOPs). The SOPs contain relatively broad guidance on how construction sites should now operate.

But are the SOPs law? And is their introduction a change in law? The starting point is that a principal contractor on a project in the United Kingdom will have health and safety obligations under the Construction (Design and Management) Regulations 2015 (CDM Regulations). These impose numerous duties, many of which are relatively broad. For example, regulation 13 states that the contractor must manage the works to ensure that they are carried out as safely as reasonably practicable. In practice, what has happened since the onset of the COVID-19 crisis is that what is considered "safe" has changed. It seems likely that compliance with the CDM Regulations requires compliance with the SOPs. Indeed, on 3 April 2020, the Health and Safety Executive, which is charged with enforcing the CDM Regulations, stated that it will seek to enforce the relevant coronavirus disease (COVID-19) measures in workplaces via enforcement and prohibition notices.

It may be arguable that the SOPs do not represent a change in law, as such, but a contractor needs to adopt them via its duties under the CDM Regulations. It is only the surrounding factual circumstances that have changed. Therefore, changes to site procedures may not be a change in law and may not even be a change to the contractor's obligations under its contract. In the context of variations, an instruction directing the contractor to adopt new measures cannot be a variation if it does not represent a change to the contractor's contractual duties. This is yet to be contested between concessionaires and contractors in the COVID-19 context.

Viet Nam

The Vietnamese standard form of power purchase agreement for wind and solar projects does not address a situation where there has been a change in law. Therefore, if a change in law resulting from COVID-19 affects a PPP contractor, it will not be entitled to any relief under the power purchase agreement, and will need to rely on any remedies that may be available under applicable laws and regulations in effect at the time or pursuant to any investment guarantee protection. Alternatively, the PPP contractor may need to attempt to negotiate a form of relief with the counterparty, the outcome of which is not assured.

2   Case Studies Regarding Compensable Delay Events

Afghanistan

In one of Afghanistan's first independent power producer projects, which was procured under a PPP-type structure, all force majeure events are compensable delay events. The PPP contractor is entitled to an extension of time to the relevant deadline, and to continued tariff payments (which covers the PPP contractor's capital expenditure costs) during the operations phase. This is regardless of the nature of the force majeure event (i.e., natural or political force majeure) or the party that is affected by the force majeure event (i.e., the PPP contractor or the customer counterparty).

The PPP contractor would also be entitled to relief if the force majeure event
- (i) causes the PPP contractor to increase its costs in constructing, modifying, repairing, operating and maintaining, and financing the PPP project; or
- (ii) decreases the gross revenue earned by the PPP contractor.
  This relief may come in the form of a one-off lumpsum payment, or an adjustment to the tariff payments for the life of the PPP project.

Therefore, if the PPP project is affected by COVID-19 and such event constitutes a force majeure event, then the PPP contractor would be entitled to an extension of time, continued tariff payment, and increased cost relief. There is an obligation on the PPP contractor to apply any insurance (e.g., business interruption insurance) it has in place to cover the tariff payments, but if such insurance does not respond, the offtaker will continue to remain responsible for the tariff payments.

The position discussed in this case study is a unique one as force majeure events, particularly natural force majeure events, are typically non-compensable delay events.

Australia

Under the Partnerships Victoria standard Project Deed, the PPP contractor may be entitled to a "compensable extension event" for a delay caused by site interface works (i.e., works performed by another contractor on the project site) or proximate interface works (i.e., works performed by a contractor outside of, but in proximity to, the project site). In each of those cases, the PPP contractor will be entitled to relief, but only if
- (i) the works being performed by the interface party are not reasonably foreseeable,
- (ii) the impact of those works is not reasonably foreseeable,
- (iii) those works are not performed in accordance with best practices, and
- (iv) the PPP contractor has complied with its obligations to coordinate with the interface party.

It follows that establishing an entitlement to claim for the conduct of an interface party may be challenging for a PPP contractor.

3   Case Study Regarding Non-Compensable Delay Events

Australia

The Partnerships Victoria standard Project Deed contemplates that the PPP contractor may enter into direct interface agreements with other contractors and operators (identified as "direct interface parties"). This means that the PPP contractor will have direct recourse to such direct interface parties in respect of interface works, which sit outside the project deed between the PPP contractor and the procuring authority. Where a breach by a direct interface party of its direct interface deed causes disruption, the PPP contractor will be entitled to an extension of time (during the development phase) or suspension of the affected obligations (during the operations phase). However, the PPP contractor will not be entitled to compensation from the procuring authority. Rather, it is implied that the PPP contractor may have separate recourse to the direct interface party pursuant to the direct interface deed.

It is foreseeable that a breach of a direct interface deed might arise because of COVID-19. For instance, a direct interface deed may provide for certain obligations to be performed within a specific time frame, which might not be achievable in a COVID-19 environment. This potential avenue of claim highlights that it is necessary to consider COVID-19 risks across the whole suite of transaction documents.

4   Case Studies Regarding Force Majeure Clauses

Australia
The Partnerships Victoria standard Project Deed, which is considered the market standard PPP position as drafted by the procuring authority in Victoria, provides that a force majeure event means the occurrence of any of the following events, which
  (i)   occurs at or in the direct vicinity of the project area;
  (ii) was not caused by the PPP contractor, the procuring agency, or their respective associates; and
  (iii) prevents the PPP contractor or the procuring agency from carrying out all or a material part of their respective obligations.

The relevant events are
  (i)   earthquake, natural disaster, bushfire, landslide, seismic activity, tsunami or mudslide;
  (ii)   winds, including sustained surface winds in excess of 118 kilometers per hour (km/h) and gusts in excess of 165 km/h during the development phase, and sustained surface winds in excess of 118 km/h and gusts in excess of 225 km/h during the operations phase (as recorded by the Bureau of Meteorology, Melbourne);
  (iii) a flood that might, at the date of the relevant deed, be expected to occur no more frequently than once in every 100 years;
  (iv)   fire, explosion, or flood caused by any of the events referred to in item (i) above;
  (v)   war, civil war, rebellion, revolution, military usurped power or mutiny, military insurrection, military commotion, or other civil commotion;
  (vi)   chemical, nuclear, or biological contamination;
  (vii) ionizing radiation or contamination by radioactivity;
  (viii) a terrorist act occurring in the project area (except to the extent whereby coverage is provided for a declared terrorist incident by operation of the Terrorism Insurance Act 2003 [Cth]); or
  (ix)   an upstream utility interruption during the operations phase.

In the occurrence of a force majeure event,
  (i)   the PPP contractor may be entitled to an extension of time (or suspension of its affected obligations during the operations phase, although the availability payment will be abated to the extent of that suspension) as well as compensation to the extent the PPP contractor is unable to pay debt amounts that are due and payable; and

(ii) the PPP contractor and the procuring agency may each terminate the project deed to the extent the force majeure event prevents the performance of the works for a continuous period exceeding 180 days.

The authors of this guidance note are yet to see a PPP contractor or procuring authority attempt to invoke these regimes in a COVID-19 context under the Partnerships Victoria standard Project Deed.

Indonesia

In PPP contracts in Indonesia (e.g., power purchase agreements with PT Perusahaan Listrik Negara [Persero]), the PPP contracts typically define an event of force majeure as any circumstance not within the reasonable control, directly or indirectly, of the affected party, but only if and to the extent that

(i) such circumstance, despite the exercise of reasonable diligence, cannot be or be caused to be prevented, avoided, or removed by such party;

(ii) such event materially adversely affects (in cost and/or time) the ability of the affected party to perform its obligations, and the affected party has taken all reasonable precautions, due care, and reasonable alternative measures to avoid the effect of such event on the affected party's ability to perform its obligations and to mitigate the consequences thereof;

(iii) such event is not the direct or indirect result of the failure of the affected party to perform any of its obligations; and

(iv) the affected party has given the counterparty prompt notice describing such event the effect thereof.

Instances of such events of force majeure include

(i) acts of war or the public enemy, whether war is declared or not;

(ii) public disorder, insurrection, rebellion, sabotage, riots, or violent demonstrations;

(iii) explosions, fires, earthquakes, floods, or other natural calamities and acts of God, or the discovery of hazardous materials or historical artefacts on the site; and

(iv) strikes or other industrial actions.

Pandemics and epidemics are not specifically listed as an event of force majeure in some of these agreements, but could nevertheless fall within the general definition of an event of force majeure.

The affected party is excused from performing its obligations, and is entitled to an equitable adjustment from the milestone schedule. Where the force majeure event affects the ability of the procuring agency to take electricity, the procuring agency continues to be liable to pay capacity payments (sometimes subject to a grace period) to the PPP contractor, which would cover the project debt repayments for the PPP contractor.

The ability of a party to terminate a PPP agreement for a prolonged force majeure event would depend on which party is affected by the force majeure event, with separate thresholds applying to prolonged force majeure event affecting the PPP contractor and affecting the procuring agency. Typically, if a prolonged force majeure event affects the PPP contractor, both parties are entitled to terminate the PPP agreement. If the prolonged force majeure event affects the procuring agency, the procuring agency would typically be the party entitled to terminate the PPP agreement because it continues to remain responsible to pay capacity payments to the PPP contractor.

Singapore

Under PPP contracts with agencies of the Government of Singapore, a party is typically excused from performance and granted an extension of time to meet the relevant deadlines if impacted by a natural force majeure event. The PPP contractor will be entitled to continued payment of the tariff to the extent that the service relating to the payment is being provided.

Natural force majeure events in Singaporean PPP contracts are typically limited to a specific list of events (rather than a general definition of what would constitute a force majeure event). Such events include

(i)   acts of war (whether declared or not), invasion, or act of a foreign enemy, in each case occurring within or involving Singapore (note that the requirement that the acts of war occur in or involve Singapore is a stricter position than many other jurisdictions that do not require such nexus to the project country);

(ii) acts of rebellion, riot, civil commotion, strikes of a political nature, an act or campaign of terrorism, or sabotage of a political nature, in each case occurring within Singapore;

(iii) lightning, earthquake, tsunami, unusual flood, storm, cyclone, typhoon, tornado, or any other natural calamity or act of God;

(iv) epidemic or plague;

(v)   strikes, work-to-rules, or "go-slows" (intentional slowdowns) (other than by employees of the affected party);

(vi) nuclear, chemical, or biological contamination (unless the affected party is the source of such contamination); and

(vii) accident, fire, or explosion (except if such accident, fire or explosion is caused by the fault or negligence of the affected party).

The PPP contractor and the procuring agency may each terminate the PPP contract if the force majeure event prevents a party from performing its obligations for a continuous period of 120 days. A PPP contractor or procuring agency has not yet attempted to invoke these regimes in a COVID-19 context in Singapore.

www.ingramcontent.com/pod-product-compliance
Lightning Source LLC
Chambersburg PA
CBHW050058220326
41599CB00045B/7454